The Division Champs

by G. Ram
illustrated by Michelle

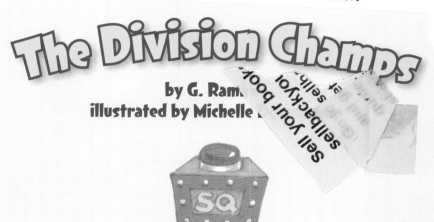

HOUGHTON MIFFLIN   BOSTON

Printed in China

ISBN 10: 0-618-89991-X
ISBN 13: 978-0-618-89991-3

9 10 11 12 0940 16 15 14 13
4500432010

In two weeks, the Midway Lions would be on the program *School Quiz* on channel 48. Chase, Asa, Tricia, and Anthony were members of the team. For the past few weeks, they had practiced for the quiz.

"I think we should practice division with remainders next," said Asa.

"What are remainders?" asked Anthony.

Tricia wrote 35 divided by 4 on the board. "I'll explain by showing you a problem," she said. "Let's say I want to divide 35, the dividend, by 4, the divisor. To start, I ask myself what I need to multiply by 4 to get an answer close to 35."

"Four times 9 is 36," answered Anthony.

"Since the dividend is 35, 9 groups of 4 are too many. But it's close, so I'll try 8. Eight is my quotient," continued Tricia. "I multiply the quotient by the divisor and get 32. When I subtract 32 from 35, I get 3. Three is the remainder."

"You're right, Asa," said Anthony. "I'm rusty on division with remainders. We'd better practice."

"I know a game we can play to practice," said Chase. "Well, it's more like a math puzzle."

"Good," said Anthony. "I love to solve puzzles."

"Okay!" said Chase. "Your job is to find the dividend. The dividend is the same for all these math statements. If the divisor is 2, the remainder is 1. If the divisor is 4, the remainder is 1. If the divisor is 5, the remainder is 1. If the divisor is 3, there is no remainder."

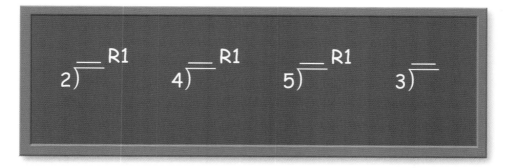

Read·Think·Write What is a remainder?

"And remember," said Chase, "the remainder is always less than the divisor."

"Let's start with what we know," said Tricia.

"The number is a multiple of 3. I know this because there is no remainder if the divisor is 3," said Anthony. "Let's try products that can be divided by 3."

"Good idea!" said Asa. "Three times 2 is 6. Six divided by 2 won't work because there is no remainder."

"You're right," said Anthony. "Maybe 9 will work."

"Nine divided by 5 won't work either because there is a remainder of 4. The remainder should be 1," said Tricia. "I think the answer is 21. It can't be 12, because 12 is divisible by 2 and 4. There isn't a remainder. It can't be 15, because 15 is divisible by 5 with no remainder. Eighteen is also divisible by 2."

"Tricia solved it!" said Chase. "Can someone make up another puzzle?"

"I've got one!" said Anthony. "How many tacos did a cook make? When 5 kids ate an equal number of the tacos, 4 tacos were left over. If 7 kids ate an equal number of tacos, there would be 3 left over. If 6 kids or 8 kids ate an equal number of tacos, there would be none left over."

"Okay," said Asa. "The dividend can be divided by both 6 and 8 with no remainder. Twelve can be divided by 6, but not by 8 with no remainder. Also eighteen can be divided by 6, but not by 8 with no remainder. Oh! I think it's 24."

"If 24 is divided by 5, there is a remainder of 4!" exclaimed Tricia. "And if 24 is divided by 7, there is a remainder of 3! Anthony, is the answer 24 tacos?"

Anthony grinned. "I'll tell you on the way to the taco shop. All this taco talk has made me hungry."

Read·Think·Write Was Asa correct? Show your work.

The day of the quiz show finally arrived. The Midway Lions felt nervous, but they did fine.

The Fairview Eagles had also been practicing. For each question Midway got right, Fairview got one right. Finally, the buzzer sounded and the game was over. Midway tied Fairview with 100 points. It was time for the tie-breaker question.

The announcer read the question. "I'm thinking of a number. If it is divided by 6, there is a remainder of 2. If it is divided by 4, the remainder is 2. If it is divided by 3, the remainder is 2. If it is divided by 2, there is no remainder."

Read·Think·Write What is the answer to the tie-breaking question?

The Midway team members smiled. Then Anthony hit the buzzer. He looked at each of his team members and then they all answered at the same time, "Fourteen!"

"That's right!" the announcer cried.

The Midway Lions had won!

After the show was over, some members of the Fairview team asked the Lions how they knew the answer. Chase got out pencil and paper and showed them how to divide with remainders.

$$
\begin{array}{r} 2 \text{ R2} \\ 6\overline{)14} \\ -12 \\ \hline 2 \end{array}
\qquad
\begin{array}{r} 3 \text{ R2} \\ 4\overline{)14} \\ -12 \\ \hline 2 \end{array}
\qquad
\begin{array}{r} 4 \text{ R2} \\ 3\overline{)14} \\ -12 \\ \hline 2 \end{array}
\qquad
\begin{array}{r} 7 \\ 2\overline{)14} \end{array}
$$

1. Which number is the divisor?

$$\begin{array}{r} 5\ R \\ 3\overline{)16} \\ -\ 15 \\ \hline 1 \end{array}$$

2. Which number is the quotient? $4\overline{)44}$

3. One of the prizes for the winning team is a box of 38 CDs. The Midway Lions team members split the CDs equally. How many CDs did each member get? How many were left over?

Activity

Visualize Use a 10 × 10 Grid and colored markers to solve:

$2\overline{)43}$ $5\overline{)47}$ $7\overline{)29}$ $3\overline{)94}$

Hint: Color rows to represent tens. Color squares to represent ones. Divide the tens by the divisor. Divide the ones by the divisor. Remember, a remainder is less than the divisor.